Charlie Bubbles 2
Smartsville!

Written by Paul Carafotes

Illustrated by Jeff Vernon

SUMMARY: The adventures continue in "Charlie Bubbles 2 Smartsville!" We follow Charlie and his magic bubble as he and his friends transform the city of ants through music and friendship.

K-4 Fun for the whole family.

Special thanks to Mark Jenest

Charlie would like to thank his family:
Mommy, Grandad, Izzy, Rampy, Joan, Aunt Suzzie
Yia Yia, Uncle Jimmy, Aunt Paula, Adam, Anastasia, Jonathan, Aunt Sophia, Demetri, Aunt Vick, Uncle Chris, James, Aunt Margo, Uncle Billy, Alexandra, Julia, Phillip, Aunt Stephanie, Uncle Roy, Charlie, Christina, Nico, Arianna

Thanks to Robert Fitzgerald, Bonnie Budd

Thanks to Steven Poffinbarger for putting Charlie in SMARTSVILLE!

Special thanks to Tai Babilonia for inspiring our new character Tai the Butterfly.

Most special thank you to my dad, Charles Carafotes, who gave me the courage and love to follow my dreams. I hope his grandson does the same.
Always remember Charlie, say "Yes" - anything is possible when you say yes!

This book is dedicated to
Liliana Ruth Gandolfini
in memory of her dad,
who was always helpful,
loving and kind.

Charlie can barely contain his joy. He's making music and blowing bubbles while pounding out a beat on his bongos. On the window sill, a caterpillar shimmies and shakes to his soulful beat.

The caterpillar dances too close to the edge and falls onto Charlie's bedroom floor.

Ants appear. Marching like soldiers, they pick up the caterpillar, then quickly move up the wall and out the window.

"Wow, talk about working together. I better try and help the little guy."

Charlie blows a bubble. It pops.

Mom enters the bedroom with Mary The Kat.
"Charlie, little bugger boo, I brought you some company."
She kisses him. "You keep an eye on him, Mary."
She squeezes the boy and is gone.

Charlie hops up and down
to get a better look out
his window.

"Hey kid, what's wrong? You got ants in your pants or something?"
"Hi Mary."
"Meow, Charlie boy. What's the latest?"
"Do you know where ants live?"
Mary purrs, "Dude, I believe they live in cool dry places under the earth."
"I mean, where exactly do they live?"
"Smartsville," says Mary.
"Smartsville? Can you take me there?" pleads Charlie.
"I'm a house kat, my man. Don't dig the outdoors." Charlie thinks...
"I have to find Teddy. He'll know what to do."

Charlie blows his magic bubble.

Excited, Mary the Kat jumps up and accidentally pushes Charlie's bubble out the window.

"Uh-oh! Dude, get back here. Your mom will be angry."

"Don't worry, I've done this before. I'm off to Smartsville. Thanks for your help, dude. Dude? Did I just say dude? Whatever."

Charlie's bubble floats high in the sky.
Paulie Pumpkin plays in a field. He sees Charlie's bubble and smiles.
Charlie lands.

"Hi Charlie. Where are you headed?"

"Smartsville, to save my caterpillar from the ants."

"Bees were one thing, but ants are stronger. They can lift like a hundred - maybe a thousand times their weight," pipes Paulie.

"He's my friend. Will you help me find him?"

"Count me in, Charlie!"

"Aww, you're the best, Paulie. Lead the way, my brave friend."

They quickly come upon a cool, clear stream and berry bushes aplenty. Hungry and thirsty, they stop to eat berries and drink from the stream. Suddenly feeling lightheaded and tired, Charlie falls fast asleep, clutching a clump of berries.

Paulie watches a long column of ants march by, carrying many things: the caterpillar, a slice of watermelon, three beetle bugs, a guitar, a drum, and a silver spoon.
Bringing up the rear is our old friend, Honey Bee.
She sees Charlie but can't buzz - the ants hold her wings closed.

Two ants climb onto Charlie. They try to pull the berries from Charlie's hand. Then Sarge-Ant wiggles his antenna under Charlie's chin, tickling him. Nada. The bubble boy will not release his grip.

"Holaaaaaaaaaa! Code rojo…we need heeeeeelllp!"
Suddenly, thousands of ants surround Charlie.

Paulie watches tiny ants carry the bubble boy off into the sunset.

Charlie, Honey Bee, and the caterpillar are seated. Sarge-Ant stands guard. The colony is bursting with activity. Giant vats simmer and boil. Ant-N prepares a feast. The caterpillar is shedding. Soon the change will come.

Charlie quietly says, "Don't you worry. We will find a way out of here." Ant-N moves closer to Charlie, feeling with her antenna. "Where am I? Why did they bring us here?" asks Charlie. "You're in Smartsville. I don't know what they have planned for you but the caterpillar is an offering to our queen."

"What about Honey Bee? Will they let her go?"
Ant-N doesn't answer.
Charlie watches every ant work together. Organized. Clean.
Marching like machines. Yet something's missing. What is it?
They all move in a joyless manner.

Ant-N appears. "It's almost time. Prepare the caterpillar stew. First, a little sweetener. Bring the Honey Bee."
"No. No, please - she's my friend. She's helpful and kind. Please don't hurt her!" Charlie pleads.
Ant-N frowns.

Teddy Hiccup hiccups then says, "Did you eat the berries and drink from the stream?"

"Yes," says Paulie. "Why?"

"It's for ants only. If anyone else attempts to eat and drink they get tired and sleepy. Then they come for you."

"Hey that's pretty smart stuff," says Paulie.

"They live in Smartsville. Duh."

"They have our friend. We must help him!" hiccups Teddy.

Back in Smartsville…

The three captured Beetles are rehearsing music, but they too are
missing something. Ant-N listens sadly.
"The queen will be very disappointed by the sound they make.
Better get them ready to add to my stew."

Charlie has an idea.
He sits at the drums and begins to play with the band.
The Beetles wiggle and shake. The ants react immediately.
Something bubbles up in them.

Ants rush the stage!

They squeal in ant-delight.
Charlie's beat is what's been missing. Aha! The ants twist and shout.
Joy spreads from antennae to antennae.
It's ant-dimonium!

Suddenly, the dancing stops.
Their powerful queen appears.
The ants part as the queen
slowly moves toward the stage.

Charlie quivers. "I meant no harm. I just wanted to play."
The queen moves closer to Charlie.
"You have been brought here not knowing your fate, yet you give us this gift."
"Gift?" Charlie asks. "They needed a beat, that's all."

"Why are you here?" asks the queen.

"To find my friends and bring them home. I humbly ask for their release." Charlie bows his head.
You could hear a bubble pop! No one ever dared ask the queen for anything before.

Just then the caterpillar sheds her cocoon, transforming into a beautiful butterfly. All the ants are humbled by the metamorphosis. The queen sees her colony and ponders a notion. The queen moves to Charlie.

"We must choose a name for her. We will call her Tai. Do you know what Tai means?" asks the queen.

"No, ma'am."

"It's Chinese. It means great."

A magic moment has occurred. "It's perfect!" says the queen.
"What about you? You ask nothing for yourself?"
"No, Your Majesty. Only that my friends are free and safe."
She looks to the Beetles, who shake from fear. She turns her powerful gaze back to Charlie.

"Would you return from time to time to make music with these Beetles?"

"Dude, that would be awesome! I mean - yes, Your Majesty."

"Then you are free to go," commands the queen. She too has changed. The colony erupts in cheers and applause.

They are saying goodbye to the ants when Teddy Hiccup and Paulie Pumpkin arrive.

"It's hocus pocus. I knew you guys would find us."

"We were upset and worried," says Teddy. Charlie gives Teddy a hug and squeeze.

"Because one squeeze will put your mind at ease," says Charlie.

"Say hello to my friend Tai. You know Honey Bee. I must get home soon or else I'll be in double trouble." Charlie Blows his bubble.

Honey Bee and Tai the Butterfly help with lift off.
Charlie waves goodbye.

"That was so exciting. So…bubble-lishious," flutters Tai.

"I learned so much," says Honey Bee.

"And what a great queen," adds Charlie. "No matter how powerful you are it takes humility and willingness to change."

Soon they fly over a field, then a familiar neighborhood. Charlie smiles warmly. And finally…

Home, sweet home.

Mary the Kat is frantic when they arrive.
"Are you kidding me, Mr. Bubbles? Do you have any idea what I've been going through since you bubbled away? Do you? Dude, that wasn't cool."
"Dude, I'm back," says Charlie. "What an adventure, you missed it Mary. Smartsville was really cool."

Charlie grabs his bongos and begins to play.
Tai the Butterfly and Honey Bee can't help themselves. They move and shake to Charlie's beat. Even Mary the Kat feels the joy and starts to dance. Charlie blows a big bubble of love and happiness.

Mom enters. "So nice to see everyone getting along. How was your afternoon, Charlie?"

Charlie smiles then says, "It was an education, mom!"

This concludes the second adventure of Charlie Bubbles.

Coming soon!
Charlie Bubbles Floats to Fenway!
To order your personally autographed
copy of the first adventure, the
critically acclaimed
'Adventures of Charlie Bubbles' visit

charliebubblesbook.com

Follow us on Twitter @charliebubbles5
Facebook/TheAdventuresOfCharlieBubbles

"One of the more imaginative and visually stunning children's books to come out this year is THE ADVENTURES OF CHARLIE BUBBLES! This sensitive and entertaining story is not only full of rich meaning for children to absorb in building solid personalities and philosophies but also is a beautiful little fable about friendship."
-- Grady Harp, Hall of Fame Reviewer,
   Amazon and Good Reads

"Charlie Bubbles is soon to be a classic.
I've read it several times and
keep re-reading it.
That's a sign that something
is good and will last."
-- James Gandolfini, Father and actor

PAUL CARAFOTES has been an award winning actor, writer and director for more than 30 years appearing in numerous movies, television shows and commercials. He has won various entertainment awards, such as best writer for his play "Beyond The Ring", as well as in writing, producing, and directing. His film "Club Soda" has won multiple awards throughout the country. "Charlie Bubbles 2 Smartsville" is Paul's second children's book in the Charlie Bubbles series. The critically acclaimed first book, "The Adventures of Charlie Bubbles" was inspired by Paul's son Charlie. You can learn more by following Paul on his "Carafotes12" Facebook page and at IMDB.com.

The author pictured with his inspiration, Charlie.

JEFF VERNON has worked as a graphic designer and illustrator for over 35 years. He has worked for numerous ad agencies, designing packaging for ATARI, and art studios creating innovative artwork including promotional key art for movies and television as well as two musical children's books. Jeff has illustrated six children's books for Veronica Lane Books and best-selling author Etan Boritzer as part of the *"What Is?"* series. This is Jeff's second collaboration with friend Paul, who he met in Hollywood in 1981. See more of Jeff's work at jeffvernon.com.